daily inspirations

of

comfort

Carolyn Larsen

christian
art gifts®

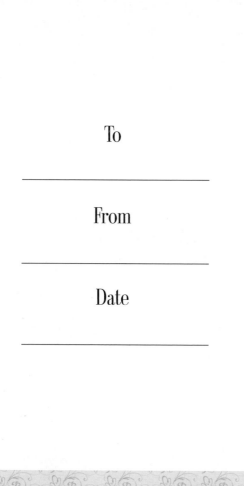

To

_____

From

_____

Date

_____

Daily Inspirations of Comfort

© 2008 Christian Art Gifts, RSA
        Christian Art Gifts Inc., IL, USA

Designed by Christian Art Gifts

Scripture quotations are taken from the *Holy Bible*, New International Version®. NIV®. Copyright © 1973, 1978, 1984 by International Bible Society. Used by permission of Zondervan Publishing House. All rights reserved.

Printed in China

ISBN 978-1-86920-555-3

08 09 10 11 12 13 14 15 16 17 – 10 9 8 7 6 5 4 3 2 1

Introduction

❧

Sometimes life is painful. Whether you are dealing with broken relationships, health problems, or changing circumstances ... life is hard. Where do you find comfort in the struggles of life?

There are a myriad of places where people look for comfort. Addictions to food, alcohol, drugs, sex and approval of others are some examples of looking for comfort in all the wrong places. Doesn't it make sense that comfort should come from the one who loves you the most and knows you the best? Sure, and that is God. He loves you completely and cares when you hurt.

Learn to find comfort from resting in the shadow of His wings.

Leaving Your Comfort Zone

What is a "comfort zone"? It's a place where you are completely at home with everything ... a place where you know what to do; what to say; and how to act. There is no challenge involved. How does it feel when you are forced out of your comfort zone? Crossing that threshold demands a risk-taking faith that believes that God will guide your every step.

Do you believe that God will guide, support and strengthen you moment by moment? Here are some suggestions of how you may find God's comfort:

- **His Word**. Scripture promises God's presence and care.
- **His voice**. God speaks by bringing a Scripture verse to mind or even through a song. Any thought that gives you comfort may very well be God speaking to you.
- **Through others**. Sometimes God uses the actions or words of others to comfort us. They are His tools at that moment in time.

God will give comfort when you need it.

Many, O Lord my God, are the wonders You have done. The things You planned for us no one can recount to You; were I to speak and tell of them, they would be too many to declare.

Psalm 40:5

If you have any encouragement from being united with Christ, if any comfort from His love, if any fellowship with the Spirit, if any tenderness and compassion, then make my joy complete by being like-minded, having the same love, being one in spirit and purpose.

Philippians 2:1-2

Let the word of Christ dwell in you richly as you teach and admonish one another with all wisdom, and as you sing psalms, hymns and spiritual songs with gratitude in your hearts to God.

Colossians 3:16

Be strong and courageous. Do not be afraid or terrified because of them, for the Lord your God goes with you; He will never leave you nor forsake you.

Deuteronomy 31:6

The Lord is my light and my salvation – whom shall I fear? The Lord is the stronghold of my life – of whom shall I be afraid?

Psalm 27:1

I sought the Lord, and He answered me; He delivered me from all my fears.

Psalm 34:4

For He chose us in Him before the creation of the world to be holy and blameless in His sight.

Ephesians 1:4

There is no fear in love. But perfect love drives out fear, because fear has to do with punishment. The one who fears is not made perfect in love.

1 John 4:18

If you're in a comfort zone,
afraid to venture out,
remember that all winners were
at one time filled with doubt.

~ *Anonymous*

❧

Dear Father, I'm so thankful that I can trust You. I believe that wherever You lead me, You will be with me; You will guide and protect me. I'm safest when I am where You want me to be. I'm excited to see what that means as You lead me through life!

Amen.

Comfort When You Hurt

Physical pain usually triumphs over whatever you are trying to do. When your body hurts it is difficult to think about anything else.

Pain is all-consuming. It's hard to care about others and it's hard to concentrate. Ongoing physical pain wears down your endurance and your attitude. Hope becomes a mere memory. Where do you turn? How do you combat the hopelessness of pain?

You must be open to receiving comfort. You cannot be comforted if you put a wall around your heart. Ask God to fill your heart with reminders of His care and concern for you. Accept comfort and help from those around you. Listen to your body – God will use it to speak to you. Your body will tell you when it needs rest or medication. Pay attention to it.

Remember that God loves you, especially in your pain. He wants you to focus your thoughts on His love and care for you.

Remember that you are not alone.

Dear friends, do not be surprised at the painful trial you are suffering, as though something strange were happening to you.

1 Peter 4:12

Cast all your anxiety on the Lord because He cares for you.

1 Peter 5:7

Why are you downcast, O my soul? Why so disturbed within me? Put your hope in God, for I will yet praise Him, my Savior.

Psalm 42:5

The LORD delights in those who fear Him, who put their hope in His unfailing love.

Psalm 147:11

The LORD appeared to us in the past, saying: "I have loved you with an everlasting love; I have drawn you with loving-kindness."

Jeremiah 31:3

For men are not cast off by the Lord forever. Though He brings grief, He will show compassion, so great is His unfailing love.

Lamentations 3:31-32

The LORD your God is with you, He is mighty to save. He will take great delight in you, He will quiet you with His love, He will rejoice over you with singing.

Zephaniah 3:17

How great is the love the Father has lavished on us, that we should be called children of God! And that is what we are!

1 John 3:1

Keep your face to the sunshine and you cannot see the shadow.

~ Helen Keller

❧

Dear Father, I can't even begin to comprehend how much You love me. I just can't wrap my mind around that. But I'm grateful ... so grateful, because I love You, too. So much.

Amen.

Comfort in Loss

Losing someone you love is one of the most difficult experiences in life. The pain and loneliness can be overwhelming. If ever comfort is needed it is in the midst of this pain – but where do you find that comfort?

Some people choose to look for comfort in things that cannot possibly quell the pain. Alcohol, work, busyness ... yet none of those things will help.

No one wants pat answers about comfort when they are struggling with the pain of great loss. Even if it just sounds like an unrealistic answer, the fact is that real comfort comes only from God. Through the precious words of Scripture, through the awareness of His presence, through the physical presence of friends and loved ones whom God Himself has placed in your life, you will experience comfort.

The truth is God does not *want* you to hurt. Therefore, look to Him, lean on Him and on those He has placed in your life.

"The Son of Man came to seek and to save what was lost."

Luke 19:10

Even though I walk through the valley of the shadow of death, I will fear no evil, for You are with me; Your rod and Your staff, they comfort me.

Psalm 23:4

"I will turn their mourning into gladness; I will give them comfort and joy instead of sorrow."

Jeremiah 31:13

The Spirit of the Sovereign LORD is on me, because the LORD has anointed me ... to comfort all who mourn.

Isaiah 61:1-2

Everything that was written in the past was written to teach us, so that through endurance and the encouragement of the Scriptures we might have hope.

Romans 15:4

Let us then approach the throne of grace with confidence, so that we may receive mercy and find grace to help us in our time of need.

Hebrews 4:16

The Lᴏʀᴅ is good to all; He has compassion on all He has made.

Psalm 145:9

I lift up my eyes to the hills – where does my help come from? My help comes from the Lᴏʀᴅ, the Maker of heaven and earth.

Psalm 121:1-2

We are continually tormented until God delivers us from misery and anguish by the remedy of His own love towards us.

~ John Calvin

❧

Dear Father, it hurts so much. I never knew I could feel so bad. Please God, heal my heart. Help me find comfort in You ... in Your Word ... in Your love.

Amen.

Comfort When Things Change

A very real kind of loss occurs when things change. Perhaps it is a job loss which leads to financial strains, or the necessity of relocating. Loss associated with change is still loss. This kind of pain sometimes results in questions being cried out to God, "Why must I go through this?" When answers are not immediately forthcoming the pain increases.

Would you like to stop the endless loop of questions and pain? There is only one way to make it stop. Turn to God; read His Word, talk to Him, wait on Him, trust Him. Sometimes change happens simply because of the world we live in or because that's how God moves us to where He wants us to be. In any of these cases, comfort comes from knowing that God is in control. Nothing happens in your life without it first passing through God's hands. He knows. He cares. He *will* comfort.

Many are the woes of the wicked, but the LORD's unfailing love surrounds the man who trusts in Him.

Psalm 32:10

"Do not let your hearts be troubled. Trust in God; trust also in Me."

John 14:1

You will keep in perfect peace him whose mind is steadfast, because he trusts in You.

Isaiah 26:3

The peace of God, which transcends all understanding, will guard your hearts and your minds in Christ Jesus.

Philippians 4:7

Let the peace of Christ rule in your hearts, since as members of one body you were called to peace.

Colossians 3:15

Now may the Lord of peace Himself give you peace at all times and in every way. The Lord be with all of you.

2 Thessalonians 3:16

How priceless is Your unfailing love! Both high and low among men find refuge in the shadow of Your wings.

Psalm 36:7

The eternal God is your refuge, and underneath are the everlasting arms.

Deuteronomy 33:27

He who rejects change is the architect of decay. The only human institution which rejects progress is the cemetery.

~ *Harold Wilson*

❧

Dear Father, thank You for Your love and care. The struggles of life are bearable because I know You love me. Your strength and comfort are what support me. Thank You for being there.

Amen.

Comfort in Illness

Fear wraps its icy hands around your heart when the doctor's report is serious – the worst possible news. Time seems to move in slow motion and normal everyday things have an unreal sense about them. Where do you find comfort in this type of situation? Where do you find hope?

Do you find comfort in prayer? Can you honestly tell God that you are afraid of the uncertainty of what this illness holds? It's okay to be afraid. In fact, it's natural. But, don't let the fear take control of your life. Pull your heart back to a centered place of trusting God ... with your very life.

In times like these many people have found comfort in a deeper, more intimate relationship with God. Of course no one wants to be ill, but the experience of illness can draw you into a sweet relationship of trust and love with God that ultimately brings the most tender comfort you have ever experienced.

"For you who revere My name, the sun of righteousness will rise with healing in its wings. And you will go out and leap like calves released from the stall."

Malachi 4:2

Be joyful in hope, patient in affliction, faithful in prayer.

Romans 12:12

Praise the LORD, O my soul, and forget not all His benefits – who forgives all your sins and heals all your diseases.

Psalm 103:2-3

Heal me, O LORD, and I will be healed; save me and I will be saved, for You are the One I praise.

Jeremiah 17:14

He who dwells in the shelter of the Most High will rest in the shadow of the Almighty. I will say of the Lord, "He is my refuge and my fortress, my God, in whom I trust."

Psalm 91:1-2

Jesus went through all the towns and villages, teaching in their synagogues, preaching the good news of the kingdom and healing every disease and sickness.

Matthew 9:35

"Peace I leave with you; My peace I give you. I do not give to you as the world gives. Do not let your hearts be troubled and do not be afraid."

John 14:27

I am convinced that neither death nor life, neither angels nor demons, neither the present nor the future, nor any powers, neither height nor depth, nor anything else in all creation, will be able to separate us from the love of God that is in Christ Jesus our Lord.

Romans 8:38-39

No matter how steep the mountain,
the Lord is going to climb it with you.
~ Helen Steiner Rice

Dear Father, okay, I'm going to be honest. Sometimes I'm scared. It's hard not to be. Help me to trust You no matter what my future holds. Help me to remember that nothing is happening to me that You don't already know about.

Amen.

Comfort in Loneliness

No one to cry with. No one to celebrate with. A feeling of loneliness tends to breed more loneliness.

Immersing yourself in the feeling that no one cares can make you withdraw even more from those who actually do care. The result is more isolation from God and all His children. Yet God has promised you His presence. Whether you sense it or not, He is with you.

To receive the comfort of His presence, it may be necessary to knock down some of the walls you've built around your heart in order to trust His promises.

However, sometimes recovering from loneliness requires the presence and comfort of people. The need to be heard, to be held is real because humans were created to be in community with a God of community.

God places people in your life who desire to be your community. Don't push them away. Thank God for them and celebrate their presence in your life.

m with you always, to the very end of

Matthew 28:20

"If anyone loves Me, he will obey My teaching. My Father will love him, and We will come to him and make Our home with him."

John 14:23

Come near to God and He will come near to you.

James 4:8

Dear children, let us not love with words or tongue but with actions and in truth.

1 John 3:18

You are no longer foreigners and aliens, but fellow citizens with God's people and members of God's household, built on the foundation of the apostles and prophets, with Christ Jesus Himself as the chief cornerstone.

Ephesians 2:19-20

Dear friends, let us love one another, for comes from God. Everyone who loves has be born of God and knows God.

I John 4:7

Just as each of us has one body with many members, and these members do not all have the same function, so in Christ we who are many form one body, and each member belongs to all the others.

Romans 12:4-5

"So do not fear, for I am with you; do not be dismayed, for I am your God. I will strengthen you and help you; I will uphold you with My righteous right hand."

Isaiah 41:10

People are lonely because they build walls instead of bridges.

~ *Joseph F. Newton*

❧

Dear Father, help me to remember that I am never really alone because You have promised to always be with me. Show me how to be friendly to others so that I may enjoy their friendship, too.

Amen.

Comfort in Service

Serving God is an honor and a privilege. But unfortunately there are times when it can feel rather thankless. Sometimes people forget to thank you for your time and effort. Sometimes churches or organizations tend to pile on the work once they discover you are serious about serving. You can quickly get buried in your service. So, where's the comfort in a situation like this?

There is one place to focus your thoughts – celebrate in joy that you are doing what God has called you to do. Being in the center of God's will and using the gifts He has given you to do His work on this planet, can give you incredible comfort.

Knowing that you are where God has placed you should bring more satisfaction than any amount of praise or appreciation from others. Concentrate on God and remember to thank Him for the opportunities He gives.

ou do, work at it with all your heart, as
he Lord, not for men, since you know
receive an inheritance from the Lord
is the Lord Christ you are serving.

Colossians 3:23-24

Being confident of this, that He who began a good work in you will carry it on to completion until the day of Christ Jesus.

Philippians 1:6

If any man builds on this foundation using gold, silver, costly stones, wood, hay or straw, his work will be shown for what it is, because the Day will bring it to light. It will be revealed with fire, and the fire will test the quality of each man's work.

1 Corinthians 3:12-13

"As long as it is day, we must do the work of Him who sent Me. Night is coming, when no one can work."

John 9:4

A curse on him who is lax in doing the LORD's work.

Jeremiah 48:10

"You will receive power when the Holy Spirit comes on you; and you will be My witnesses in Jerusalem, and in all Judea and Samaria, and to the ends of the earth."

Acts 1:8

All Scripture is God-breathed and is useful for teaching, rebuking, correcting and training in righteousness, so that the man of God may be thoroughly equipped for every good work.

2 Timothy 3:16-17

Those who are wise will shine like the brightness of the heavens, and those who lead many to righteousness, like the stars for ever and ever.

Daniel 12:3

The world is filled with willing people;
some willing to work,
the rest willing to let them.

~ Robert Frost

Dear Father, I needed to hear this. Help me to remember that I'm working for You. Thank You for the privilege of using my gifts and talents for You. Thank You that I can serve You. I pray for the strength and energy to serve with all my might!

Amen.

Comfort in Growth

Growing pains hurt – whether they are physical or spiritual – but the spiritual ones are often hardest to deal with. They involve pain that can't be treated with an over-the-counter pain reliever.

It's important to realize that these growing pains have a purpose in your life. Just as physical growing pains mean that your body, in fact your bones, are growing you toward adulthood, spiritual growing pains are maturing you, too. Spiritual growth happens at a deeper level; in the midst of crises and pain. Dependence on God is necessary, prayer becomes a priority, and you are moved along the path toward becoming more like Christ.

While growth often hurts, it is not pain without purpose. Remember to turn to God during these times. Spend time in prayer, meditation and reading His Word. Allow Him to grow you and take comfort in knowing that this time of hardship will pass, and when it does your faith will be stronger and deeper.

God is able to make all grace abound to you, so that in all things at all times, having all that you need, you will abound in every good work.

2 Corinthians 9:8

To Him who is able to do immeasurably more than all we ask or imagine, according to His power that is at work within us, to Him be glory in the church and in Christ Jesus throughout all generations, forever and ever!

Ephesians 3:20-21

Do your best to present yourself to God as one approved, a workman who does not need to be ashamed and who correctly handles the word of truth.

2 Timothy 2:15

The word of God is living and active. Sharper than any double-edged sword, it penetrates even to dividing soul and spirit, joints and marrow; it judges the thoughts and attitudes of the heart.

Hebrews 4:12

Listen to advice and accept instruction, and in the end you will be wise.

Proverbs 19:20

Watch your life and doctrine closely. Persevere in them, because if you do, you will save both yourself and your hearers.

I Timothy 4:16

Speaking the truth in love, we will in all things grow up into Him who is the Head, that is, Christ.

Ephesians 4:15

"When you pass through the waters, I will be with you; and when you pass through the rivers, they will not sweep over you. When you walk through the fire, you will not be burned; the flames will not set you ablaze. For I am the LORD, your God, the Holy One of Israel, your Savior."

Isaiah 43:2-3

Growth is the only evidence of life.
~ *John Henry Newman*

❧

Dear Father, this time of growth hurts. Help me to remember that good things will come from it. Help my faith to grow stronger and deeper and my dependence on You to be more secure. Thank You for loving me enough to grow me.

Amen.

Comfort in Prayer

A quiet afternoon spent talking with a good friend is such a pleasure. Sharing secrets, stories about your lives, jokes that only the two of you understand, things that worry or concern you, and things you are celebrating. Regular conversation deepens your friendship as you get to know each other better and begin trusting one another at a deeper level.

Prayer is like that too. Prayer is conversation with God. Regular conversation with Him where you share the things on your heart – the people and things you care about – deepens your relationship with Him. It's a comfort to be able to talk to God about the things that concern you as well as the things that bring you joy.

You can talk to God about things you don't understand and share your joys. The more you pray, the more your heart will become aligned with God's heart.

What could be more comforting than knowing you are mirroring the heart of God?

This is the confidence we have in approaching God: that if we ask anything according to His will, He hears us. And if we know that He hears us – whatever we ask – we know that we have what we asked of Him.

I John 5:14-15

What other nation is so great as to have their gods near them the way the Lord our God is near us whenever we pray to Him?

Deuteronomy 4:7

"If My people, who are called by My name, will humble themselves and pray and seek My face and turn from their wicked ways, then will I hear from heaven and will forgive their sin and will heal their land."

2 Chronicles 7:14

"When you pray, go into your room, close the door and pray to your Father, who is unseen. Then your Father, who sees what is done in secret, will reward you."

Matthew 6:6

In the same way, the Spirit helps us in our weakness. We do not know what we ought to pray for, but the Spirit Himself intercedes for us with groans that words cannot express.

Romans 8:26

Pray continually.

I Thessalonians 5:17

Confess your sins to each other and pray for each other so that you may be healed. The prayer of a righteous man is powerful and effective.

James 5:16

The eyes of the Lord are on the righteous and His ears are attentive to their prayer, but the face of the Lord is against those who do evil.

I Peter 3:12

The Lord will either calm the storm or let it rage while He calms you.

~ Anonymous

Dear Father, I'm so thankful for the privilege of prayer. What a blessing to be able to talk with You anytime about anything and anyone. I know that You care for me and hear my prayers. Thank You for loving me!

Amen.

Comfort in Confusion

There's no doubt about the fact that life sometimes gets confusing. You may be so busy that you feel as though you're running in circles and you don't even have time to think. Choices and decisions loom before you and confusion reigns. How do you know which path to take? How do you know what to do? How do you know what God wants you to do?

Confusion racing through your mind and heart can be tiring and overwhelming. Where do you find comfort in the midst of so much confusion?

Scripture tells us that God is not the author of confusion, so comfort will come from Him. He has a plan for your life. He knows what it is and He will guide you into it. However, you have a responsibility. Be still before God, listen for His voice, spend time in His Word. Allow Him the time and quiet moments to be able to guide you.

Find comfort in the midst of confusion by hearing the still, calm voice of God.

"Be still, and know that I am God; I will be exalted among the nations, I will be exalted in the earth."

Psalm 46:10

Be still before the LORD, all mankind, because He has roused Himself from His holy dwelling.

Zechariah 2:13

Jesus Christ is the same yesterday and today and forever.

Hebrews 13:8

"I will instruct you and teach you in the way you should go; I will counsel you and watch over you."

Psalm 32:8

God did not give us a spirit of timidity, but a spirit of power, of love and of self-discipline.

2 Timothy 1:7

We know that in all things God works for the good of those who love Him, who have been called according to His purpose.

Romans 8:28

God is not a God of disorder but of peace.

1 Corinthians 14:33

He who walks with the wise grows wise, but a companion of fools suffers harm.

Proverbs 13:20

I do not want the peace that passeth understanding. I want the understanding which bringeth peace.

~ Helen Keller

❧

Dear Father, sometimes confusion seems to reign in my life. But I know that confusion doesn't come from You – it's either because of my own doing or Satan is trying to keep me from being obedient to You. Help me to stay close to You and to follow Your guidance. Thank You, Lord, for making my path clear.

Amen.

Comfort in Failure

It's easy to give pat "Sunday school" answers about comfort in failure. Things like, "At least you tried" or "Failure makes you appreciate the work and persistence that brings success." However, when you're struggling with the pain of failure, the last thing you want to hear is clichéd answers.

What you want is to know that someone recognizes your pain. You want someone to empathize with you; to just sit quietly with you or take you out for ice cream – whatever you need.

Of course, you know in your heart that God cares about how you feel. He said it in His Word. God is love. God loves you. He sent His Son to die for you. He cares about how you feel right now. Look around you at the people God has placed in your life. They aren't there by accident. Allow God to comfort you through them. Understand that God's comfort comes in different forms.

God is not unjust; He will not forget your work and the love you have shown Him as you have helped His people and continue to help them.

Hebrews 6:10

"My grace is sufficient for you, for My power is made perfect in weakness."

2 Corinthians 12:9

I can do everything through Him who gives me strength.

Philippians 4:13

Be strong and courageous, and do the work. Do not be afraid or discouraged, for the Lord God, my God, is with you. He will not fail you or forsake you until all the work for the service of the temple of the Lord is finished.

1 Chronicles 28:20

If we endure, we will also reign with Him.

2 Timothy 2:12

Commit to the LORD whatever you do, and your plans will succeed.

Proverbs 16:3

With God we will gain the victory, and He will trample down our enemies.

Psalm 60:12

Not that we are competent in ourselves to claim anything for ourselves, but our competence comes from God.

2 Corinthians 3:5

Where hope grows, miracles blossom.

~ Elna Rae

❧

Dear Father, I guess no one likes to fail. I sure don't. But I'm thankful that even in failure I'm reminded to depend only on You. Any success I have in anything is because of You. Thank You for Your strength, help and courage in my life.

Amen.

Comfort in Fear

Icy hands wrap around your heart; your breath comes in short, shallow bursts; a knot in the pit of your stomach grows larger and heavier with each passing minute ... fear has taken control of your body. What do you most fear? Death? Pain? Embarrassment? Whatever fear tops your list, it is consuming and powerful.

What do you do? How do you escape this terror? Sometimes facing your fear head on diffuses its power over you. Sometimes talking about it with someone you trust puts your fear in perspective. However, the most powerful antidote to fear is love, and the greatest love comes from God. He loves you and will protect and strengthen you in the face of your fear.

Tell Him what you fear. Ask Him to give you the strength to overcome it. Draw strength from the strongest power you will ever know – God's incredible love.

The Almighty is beyond our reach and exalted in power; in His justice and great righteousness, He does not oppress. Therefore, men revere Him, for does He not have regard for all the wise in heart?

Job 37:23-24

You are a chosen people, a royal priesthood, a holy nation, a people belonging to God, that you may declare the praises of Him who called you out of darkness into His wonderful light.

1 Peter 2:9

Praise be to the LORD, for He showed His wonderful love to me when I was in a besieged city.

Psalm 31:21

The eyes of the LORD range throughout the earth to strengthen those whose hearts are fully committed to Him.

2 Chronicles 16:9

This is love: not that we loved God, but that He loved us and sent His Son as an atoning sacrifice for our sins.

1 John 4:10

"As the Father has loved Me, so have I loved you. Now remain in My love."

John 15:9

Hope does not disappoint us, because God has poured out His love into our hearts by the Holy Spirit, whom He has given us.

Romans 5:5

"Even to your old age and gray hairs I am He, I am He who will sustain you. I have made you and I will carry you; I will sustain you and I will rescue you."

Isaiah 46:4

The greatest happiness of life is the conviction that we are loved – loved for ourselves, or rather, loved in spite of ourselves.

~Victor Hugo

❧

Dear Father, knowing that You love me is what gets me through the times when I'm terrified. Your love is an anchor that holds me firmly. Thank You for that love. Thank You for never leaving me alone.

Amen.

Comfort in Grief

Grief is a strange emotion. It overwhelms and overshadows everything. It may seem that your struggle with grief has ended and you finally have victory, but suddenly, without warning, it comes crashing down on you once again. Grief seems to change the very molecules of your being. Finding (or even accepting) comfort in this place of pain is difficult. In fact, sometimes you must choose to allow someone to come close enough to offer comfort. You may even have to choose to allow God that close to your heart again.

Grief is sometimes interwoven with disappointment that God didn't do what you desired – like fix a broken marriage or heal a sick loved one.

Comfort in grief comes only when you realize that God truly knows best. He sees the bigger picture of your life and future. God knows that some things hurt you. Does He care? Of course He does. He loves you dearly.

The Sovereign LORD will wipe away the tears from all faces; He will remove the disgrace of His people from all the earth.

Isaiah 25:8

"I tell you the truth, whoever hears My word and believes Him who sent Me has eternal life and will not be condemned; he has crossed over from death to life."

John 5:24

He was despised and rejected by men, a Man of sorrows, and familiar with suffering.

Isaiah 53:3

In bringing many sons to glory, it was fitting that God, for whom and through whom everything exists, should make the author of their salvation perfect through suffering.

Hebrews 2:10

He Himself bore our sins in His body on the tree, so that we might die to sins and live for righteousness; by His wounds you have been healed.

1 Peter 2:24

The Lamb at the center of the throne will be their Shepherd; He will lead them to springs of living water. And God will wipe away every tear from their eyes.

Revelation 7:17

In this you greatly rejoice, though now for a little while you may have had to suffer grief in all kinds of trials.

I Peter 1:6

"Where, O death, is your victory? Where, O death, is your sting?" The sting of death is sin, and the power of sin is the law. But thanks be to God! He gives us the victory through our Lord Jesus Christ.

I Corinthians 15:55-56

God is not a deceiver, that He should offer to support us, and then, when we lean upon Him, should slip away from us.
~ *Saint Augustine*

❧

Dear Father, my heart is aching. I didn't know it could hurt so badly. I'm so thankful to know that You have victory over death. I'm thankful for the promise of eternity when I will be reunited with my loved one. Thank You for Your comfort and strength that You give me to help get me through this grief.

Amen.

Comfort in Temptation

Temptation is tough because you may not want the people around you to know what you're struggling with. The things that tempt you may be embarrassing or may take you out of the realm of what is "accepted" by fellow Christians. If you feel like you can't talk to others about your struggle, from where will your help come?

Jesus understands temptation. He experienced intense temptation for forty days. What you are experiencing is nothing new to Him. Remember how Jesus responded to temptation? He quoted Scripture. If it worked for Jesus, it can also work for you. Immerse yourself in God's Word. Search for Scripture verses on strength and love. Repeat them to yourself over and over.

Your comfort will come from God's Word and the knowledge that Jesus faced temptation as well, but never gave in.

Submit yourselves, then, to God. Resist the devil, and he will flee from you.

James 4:7

To Him who is able to keep you from falling and to present you before His glorious presence without fault and with great joy – to the only God our Savior be glory, majesty, power and authority, through Jesus Christ our Lord, before all ages, now and forevermore! Amen.

Jude 24-25

You, dear children, are from God and have overcome them, because the One who is in you is greater than the one who is in the world.

I John 4:4

I have hidden Your word in my heart that I might not sin against You.

Psalm 119:11

Consider it pure joy, my brothers, whenever you face trials of many kinds, because you know that the testing of your faith develops perseverance.

James 1:2-3

Finally, be strong in the Lord and in His mighty power. Put on the full armor of God so that you can take your stand against the devil's schemes.

Ephesians 6:10-11

Be self-controlled and alert. Your enemy the devil prowls around like a roaring lion looking for someone to devour. Resist him, standing firm in the faith, because you know that your brothers throughout the world are undergoing the same kind of sufferings.

1 Peter 5:8-9

Do not let this Book of the Law depart from your mouth; meditate on it day and night, so that you may be careful to do everything written in it. Then you will be prosperous and successful.

Joshua 1:8

All the water in the world, however hard it tries, can never sink the smallest ship unless it gets inside, and all the evil in the world, the blackest kind of sin, can never hurt you in the least, unless you let it in.

~ *Anonymous*

Dear Father, temptation is no fun. I need Your strength to stand firm. Please bring Scripture to mind when I feel tempted. Strengthen me and remind me of Your presence that is with me every moment.

Amen.

Comfort in Rejection

Putting yourself "out there" with another person is when you offer your friendship or even your heart to someone. There is no doubt that it's a vulnerable position to be in. Hopefully, your friendship or love is returned, but this is not always the case.

Rejection is painful and can bruise your self-image. What do you do when you've offered your heart to someone who turns and walks away? How do you find comfort?

There is no denying that rejection hurts or that Satan will use the experience of rejection to try to sink you even deeper into depression.

Your only hope for recovery is to focus your mind on positive things. Focus on the people in your life who love you. Focus on God's promise to always be with you. Focus on your worth in God's eyes.

Just because one person walks away from you does not mean everyone else will too.

Though I walk in the midst of trouble, You preserve my life; You stretch out Your hand against the anger of my foes, with Your right hand You save me.

Psalm 138:7

The LORD is good, a refuge in times of trouble. He cares for those who trust in Him.

Nahum 1:7

Though my father and mother forsake me, the LORD will receive me.

Psalm 27:10

The LORD Himself goes before you and will be with you; He will never leave you nor forsake you. Do not be afraid; do not be discouraged.

Deuteronomy 31:8

"A new command I give you: Love one another. As I have loved you, so you must love one another."

John 13:34

For the sake of His great name the L ORD will not reject His people, because the L ORD was pleased to make you His own.

I Samuel 12:22

The God of all grace, who called you to His eternal glory in Christ, after you have suffered a little while, will Himself restore you and make you strong, firm and steadfast.

I Peter 5:10

"No one will be able to stand up against you all the days of your life. As I was with Moses, so I will be with you; I will never leave you nor forsake you."

Joshua 1:5

*Giving someone all your love
is never an assurance that they'll
love you back. Don't expect love in
return, just wait for it to grow in their
hearts, but if it doesn't, be content
it grew in yours.*

~ *Anonymous*

*Dear Father, please remind me how much I
mean to You. It's hard to focus on that when
my heart is hurting so much. Thank You for
Your Word that tells me I matter to You.
Thank You for the comfort of Your love. Help
me to look forward to tomorrow instead of
focusing on the pain of today.*

Amen.

Comfort and Joy

Comfort and joy definitely go together. Comfort brings joy and joy brings comfort. But here's the trick. Sometimes when you're in the place where you need comfort, the last thing you want is to be around someone who is really perky, right? A little joy is okay, but when a person is over the top happy *all the time*, do you sometimes want to suggest that she "happy down" a little.

Sometimes in order to receive comfort, it is necessary to let the walls of resistance down and be open to the joy in someone else's heart. That joy can actually be a bit contagious and can begin to heal the wounds that cause you so much pain.

Allow the joy in another person's heart to be the tender medicine you so badly need. It may just be that God will choose that joy to help you rise from the pit you've sunken into.

The joy of the Lord is your strength.

Nehemiah 8:10

Rejoice in the Lord always. I will say it again: Rejoice!

Philippians 4:4

You have made known to me the path of life; You will fill me with joy in Your presence, with eternal pleasures at Your right hand.

Psalm 16:11

I will rejoice in the Lord, I will be joyful in God my Savior.

Habakkuk 3:18

The fruit of the Spirit is love, joy, peace, patience, kindness, goodness, faithfulness, gentleness and self-control.

Galatians 5:22-23

I know that I will remain, and I will continue with all of you for your progress and joy in the faith, so that through my being with you again your joy in Christ Jesus will overflow on account of me.

Philippians 1:25-26

Be joyful always.

I Thessalonians 5:16

If you have any encouragement from being united with Christ, if any comfort from His love, if any fellowship with the Spirit, if any tenderness and compassion, then make my joy complete by being like-minded, having the same love, being one in spirit and purpose.

Philippians 2:1-2

*Do not look for rest in any pleasure,
because you were not created for pleasure:
you were created for joy. And if you do
not know the difference between pleasure
and joy, you have not yet begun to live.*

~ Thomas Merton

Dear Father, I need some joy in my life. Help me to be open to the joy that others can share with me. Help me to find comfort in that. I pray, too, Father that I may find comfort and joy in You and Your Word. Help me to trust You enough to find joy there.

Amen.

Comfort from Burdens

The burden of concern or fear is like a weight pressing down on you. The heavier the burden, the more difficult it is to get up in the morning; to have energy for the day; to care about anything else.

Often when you are carrying a burden you feel as though no one else understands what you're going through, and that may be true. However, even if those around you don't understand your problem, they still care. Even more than that, God understands and He cares.

The temptation to feel that you're alone in the world is magnified by Satan's attempts to beat you down and make you feel abandoned. Do not let him succeed. Reach out to God through the comfort and blessing of His Word.

Let your heart be soothed by your favorite hymns that focus your thoughts on Him.

Reach out to those around you and accept the comfort of their company and care. Remember – you are not alone.

We are God's fellow workers; you are God's field, God's building.

I Corinthians 3:9

I press on toward the goal to win the prize for which God has called me heavenward in Christ Jesus.

Philippians 3:14

"Watch and pray so that you will not fall into temptation. The spirit is willing, but the body is weak."

Matthew 26:41

In my distress I called to the Lord, and He answered me. From the depths of the grave I called for help, and You listened to my cry.

Jonah 2:2

"Come to Me, all you who are weary and burdened, and I will give you rest."

Matthew 11:28

Humble yourselves, therefore, under God's mighty hand, that He may lift you up in due time. Cast all your anxiety on Him because He cares for you.

I Peter 5:6-7

Cast your cares on the LORD and He will sustain you; He will never let the righteous fall.

Psalm 55:22

Let us not become weary in doing good, for at the proper time we will reap a harvest if we do not give up.

Galatians 6:9

God does not comfort us to make us comfortable, but to make us comforters.

~John Henry Jowett

❧

Dear Father, I need the encouragement of Your Word. Thank You for the reminders of Your presence with me. Thank You for Your strength that fills me with the energy to keep on going.

Amen.

Comfort in Persecution

Persecution is when you're punished or "picked on" for doing or believing something that you do not think is wrong. It's not persecution if you are punished because you murdered someone or stole something. It's persecution if you are punished simply because you believe in God. Persecution is not an easy thing to experience.

However, persecution because of faith in God is not a new thing. There are examples in Scripture of those who were hurt and even killed for their faith in God, and there have been many more who were persecuted for their faith since biblical times. Where is the comfort in that?

God rewards those whose faith stands solid in difficult times. If you are being persecuted in any way because of your faith, be assured that He knows about it. He will see you through this difficult time and He will reward you for your faith and courage.

Restore to me the joy of Your salvation and grant me a willing spirit, to sustain me.

Psalm 51:12

We say with confidence, "The Lord is my helper; I will not be afraid. What can man do to me?"

Hebrews 13:6

The LORD is the everlasting God, the Creator of the ends of the earth. He will not grow tired or weary, and His understanding no one can fathom. He gives strength to the weary and increases the power of the weak. Even youths grow tired and weary, and young men stumble and fall; but those who hope in the LORD will renew their strength. They will soar on wings like eagles; they will run and not grow weary, they will walk and not be faint.

Isaiah 40:28-31

Wait for the LORD; be strong and take heart and wait for the LORD.

Psalm 27:14

Do not be anxious about anything, but in everything, by prayer and petition, with thanksgiving, present your requests to God. And the peace of God, which transcends all understanding, will guard your hearts and your minds in Christ Jesus.

Philippians 4:6-7

It has been granted to you on behalf of Christ not only to believe on Him, but also to suffer for Him, since you are going through the same struggle you saw I had, and now hear that I still have.

Philippians 1:29-30

"Do not be afraid of what you are about to suffer. I tell you, the devil will put some of you in prison to test you, and you will suffer persecution for ten days. Be faithful, even to the point of death, and I will give you the crown of life."

Revelation 2:10

Consider the postage stamp:
its usefulness consists in the ability to
stick to one thing until it gets there.

~ Josh Billings

Dear Father, persecution scares me – but God, I want to be worthy of You. As I face persecution on any level for my faith in You, I pray for Your strength and courage to hold me up and for Your power to go before me. Help me, Father, to keep living strong for You. Help me to be worthy of You.

Amen.

The Comforter Is Always Present

Have you ever secretly wondered whether God actually hears your prayers? Have you wondered if He cares about what you're going through; about the problems you have? Do those times when it seems that God isn't hearing, let alone answering, leave you feeling alone or even abandoned by this One who supposedly loves you more than any other?

Don't write off God's love and concern. Remember, Christ promised to be with His children always, "Surely, I am with you always" (Matthew 28:20). What God promises is set in stone. He never goes back on a promise, so you can know that He is with you even if you can't sense His presence at the moment.

So how do you get past this lonely feeling? Read His Word and trust what He says. He is with you and He always will be. Believe it.

"Heaven and earth will pass away, but My words will never pass away."

Matthew 24:35

All Your words are true; all Your righteous laws are eternal.

Psalm 119:160

Let the word of Christ dwell in you richly as you teach and admonish one another with all wisdom, and as you sing psalms, hymns and spiritual songs with gratitude in your hearts to God.

Colossians 3:16

Fix these words of mine in your hearts and minds; tie them as symbols on your hands and bind them on your foreheads.

Deuteronomy 11:18

The unfolding of Your words gives light; it gives understanding to the simple.

Psalm 119:130

"Surely I am with you always, to the very end of the age."

Matthew 28:20

"I will ask the Father, and He will give you another Counselor to be with you forever – the Spirit of truth."

John 14:16-17

"In My Father's house are many rooms; if it were not so, I would have told you. I am going there to prepare a place for you. And if I go and prepare a place for you, I will come back and take you to be with Me that you also may be where I am."

John 14:2-3

You can see God from anywhere if your mind is set to love and obey Him.

~ A. W. Tozer

❧

Dear Father, what a comfort to know that You are always with me and always will be. I need not fear anything that life brings because I know I am never alone. Thank You for Your love and presence in my life.

Amen.

Comfort in Sickness

Sickness is a normal part of life. However, being sick for a long period of time is exhausting. It wears down your attitude and depletes your energy. The longer the sickness goes on, the more it colors everything else in your life. It becomes difficult to enjoy being with people, difficult to accept help, difficult to feel encouraged. The only thing that is really easy is the tendency to develop a negative outlook on everything.

Is there any hope of comfort when you've suffered from sickness for a long time? The simple answer is "yes". Comfort is always possible.

Remember that God loves you so much that He sent His only Son for you. That's a lot of love. Someone who loves you that much must care about the sickness you're dealing with. He will walk beside you through this time just as He does through good times. That's what love does. Never doubt it.

Jesus went through all the towns and villages, teaching in their synagogues, preaching the good news of the kingdom and healing every disease and sickness.

Matthew 9:35

"For God so loved the world that He gave His one and only Son, that whoever believes in Him shall not perish but have eternal life."

John 3:16

Is any one of you sick? He should call the elders of the church to pray over him and anoint him with oil in the name of the Lord. And the prayer offered in faith will make the sick person well; the Lord will raise him up.

James 5:14-15

"I have loved you with an everlasting love; I have drawn you with loving-kindness."

Jeremiah 31:3

He was pierced for our transgressions, He was crushed for our iniquities; the punishment that brought us peace was upon Him, and by His wounds we are healed.

Isaiah 53:5

I will never forget Your precepts, for by them You have preserved my life.

Psalm 119:93

"Lord, if You are willing, You can make me clean." Jesus reached out His hand and touched the man. "I am willing," He said. "Be clean." And immediately the leprosy left him.

Luke 5:12-13

"My grace is sufficient for you, for My power is made perfect in weakness."

2 Corinthians 12:9

*The love of God is like the
Amazon River flowing down
to water one daisy.*

~ *Anonymous*

Dear Father, being sick gets tiresome. I long to feel well and energized again. Father, I ask for Your healing in my body. Until that comes, I ask for Your strength to sustain me and for my trust in You to stay strong.

Amen.

Comfort and Hope

Imagine darkness so thick that you can't see your own hand in front of your face. Darkness that covers all light, all efforts to guide and direct. Total darkness is consuming and terrifying. In such complete blackness, one thin sliver of light is the equivalent of hope. It provides a direction to look towards and the hope of an escape from the darkness. It is quite simply, a comfort.

When the circumstances of life weigh heavily on you, drowning out all joy and hope, what do you do? Some people turn their faces to the wall and hide, some run around blindly, and others become completely immobile.

Are you able to look around for the thin sliver of light that offers hope and comfort in the darkness? It is always there – in the tenderness and promise of God's Word, in the words of a song, in the smile of a friend. God always gives that hope. Look for it. Find comfort in it.

Those who hope in the LORD will renew their strength. They will soar on wings like eagles; they will run and not grow weary, they will walk and not be faint.

Isaiah 40:31

"Call to Me and I will answer you and tell you great and unsearchable things you do not know."

Jeremiah 33:3

Cast your cares on the LORD and He will sustain you; He will never let the righteous fall.

Psalm 55:22

"I know the plans I have for you," declares the LORD, "plans to prosper you and not to harm you, plans to give you hope and a future."

Jeremiah 29:11

Forgetting what is behind and straining toward what is ahead, I press on toward the goal to win the prize for which God has called me heavenward in Christ Jesus.

Philippians 3:13-14

Faith is being sure of what we hope for and certain of what we do not see.

Hebrews 11:1

You have been my hope, O Sovereign LORD, my confidence since my youth.

Psalm 71:5

In this hope we were saved. But hope that is seen is no hope at all. Who hopes for what he already has? But if we hope for what we do not yet have, we wait for it patiently.

Romans 8:24-25

*God does not give us everything we want,
but He does fulfill all His promises ...
leading us along the best
and straightest paths to holiness.*

~ Dietrich Bonhoeffer

Dear Father, hope is what keeps me going. Hope that things will get better. Hope that I will obey more. Hope for eternity with You. Thank You that because of You and Your work throughout history and in my life, I can have hope.

Amen.

Comfort by God's Faithfulness

People sometimes disappoint us and unfortunately we disappoint people too. We try not to, but we're not perfect. Whether it is because of forgotten promises, broken commitments or just misunderstandings, we sometimes do disappoint one another. God, on the other hand, never disappoints.

You can anchor your faith in the fact that what God says in His Word is true and He will never act in a way that is contrary to His Word. God is faithful. That means you can depend on Him no matter what.

Read through the Old Testament and see how often God's people disobeyed or disappointed Him. Did God turn away from them? No. His love is deep and constant. Understanding that, you can know that even if you have disobeyed or disappointed Him, He is still faithfully waiting for you to turn back to Him. What a comfort that is!

The Word became flesh and made His dwelling among us. We have seen His glory, the glory of the One and Only, who came from the Father, full of grace and truth.

John 1:14

"As the rain and the snow come down from heaven, and do not return to it without watering the earth and making it bud and flourish, so that it yields seed for the sower and bread for the eater, so is My word that goes out from My mouth: It will not return to Me empty, but will accomplish what I desire and achieve the purpose for which I sent it."

Isaiah 55:10-11

Know therefore that the LORD your God is God; He is the faithful God, keeping His covenant of love to a thousand generations of those who love Him and keep His commands.

Deuteronomy 7:9

The word of the LORD is right and true; He is faithful in all He does.

Psalm 33:4

May God Himself, the God of peace, sanctify you through and through. May your whole spirit, soul and body be kept blameless at the coming of our Lord Jesus Christ. The One who calls you is faithful and He will do it.

I Thessalonians 5:23-24

I will sing of the Lord's great love forever; with my mouth I will make Your faithfulness known through all generations.

Psalm 89:1

I lift up my eyes to the hills – where does my help come from? My help comes from the Lord, the Maker of heaven and earth. He will not let your foot slip – He who watches over you will not slumber; indeed, He who watches over Israel will neither slumber nor sleep.

Psalm 121:1-4

Have no fear of sudden disaster or of the ruin that overtakes the wicked, for the Lord will be your confidence and will keep your foot from being snared.

Proverbs 3:25-26

When God would make His name known to mankind, He could find no better word than "I AM". "I am that I am," says God, "I change not." Everyone and everything else measures from that fixed point.

~ A. W. Tozer

Dear Father, so much of life is uncertain. So many relationships come and go over the years. The one true thing; the one thing I can always count on, is You. Thank You for being the same yesterday, today and tomorrow. I feel secure because of You.

Amen.

Comfort in Depression

Once in a while everyone experiences depression. It doesn't usually last very long or become too consuming. If it does, of course, professional help may be needed. But in the normal course of life there are times when mild depression hits. The danger you should be aware of is not to sink into the depression and allow yourself to wallow in it. When that happens the dark cloud only grows bigger and life grows darker.

Instead of sinking into a pit of depression, how do you escape its grip? Change your focus. Instead of focusing on the cause of your depression or playing out possible scenarios in your mind, turn your mind to positive thoughts. Review Scripture verses on God's love and care. Being around other people can help you focus on something besides yourself and your problem.

Let the people God has placed around you offer comfort and support. God cares about whatever you are going through. Let Him help you escape the darkness.

These are written that you may believe that Jesus is the Christ, the Son of God, and that by believing you may have life in His name.

John 20:31

It is God who works in you to will and to act according to His good purpose.

Philippians 2:13

God demonstrates His own love for us in this: While we were still sinners, Christ died for us.

Romans 5:8

Finally, brothers, whatever is true, whatever is noble, whatever is right, whatever is pure, whatever is lovely, whatever is admirable – if anything is excellent or praiseworthy – think about such things.

Philippians 4:8

Trust in the Lord with all your heart and lean not on your own understanding; in all your ways acknowledge Him, and He will make your paths straight.

Proverbs 3:5-6

The LORD will fulfill His purpose for me; Your love, O LORD, endures forever – do not abandon the works of Your hands.

Psalm 138:8

We are hard pressed on every side, but not crushed; perplexed, but not in despair; persecuted, but not abandoned; struck down, but not destroyed.

2 Corinthians 4:8-9

You will keep in perfect peace him whose mind is steadfast, because he trusts in You.

Isaiah 26:3

God keeps open house
for hungry sinners.
~ *Thomas Watson*

❧

Dear Father, You are my lifeline. You are what pulls me from the pit of depression. Thank You for being steady and secure. Thank You for being my anchor. Help me to focus my thoughts on You and not on those things that will drag me back into the pit.

Amen.

Comfort in Conflict

Serious conflict between you and a friend or a loved one colors pretty much all of life. When this happens to you, do you find that the broken relationship is all you can think about? Whether you're thinking about how to fix things or having ongoing arguments in your mind (which you always seem to win), it is difficult to focus on other things.

Broken relationships seldom heal themselves. One person has to take the first step. Sitting down together and talking through the issues with an attitude reflecting the wisdom of "Be quick to listen and slow to speak" is the best attack.

Talking ... and listening, will help both of you work through the problem. Hearing one another's opinions and feelings shows you value each other.

Relief from conflict comes by handling the situation maturely. Comfort comes from a relationship restored.

Everyone should be quick to listen, slow to speak and slow to become angry, for man's anger does not bring about the righteous life that God desires.

James 1:19

Love is patient, love is kind. It does not envy, it does not boast, it is not proud. It is not rude, it is not self-seeking, it is not easily angered, it keeps no record of wrongs. Love does not delight in evil but rejoices with the truth. It always protects, always trusts, always hopes, always perseveres.

1 Corinthians 13:4-7

A gentle answer turns away wrath, but a harsh word stirs up anger.

Proverbs 15:1

"In your anger do not sin": Do not let the sun go down while you are still angry, and do not give the devil a foothold.

Ephesians 4:26-27

"If you forgive men when they sin against you, your heavenly Father will also forgive you. But if you do not forgive men their sins, your Father will not forgive your sins."

Matthew 6:14-15

A patient man has great understanding, but a quick-tempered man displays folly.

Proverbs 14:29

Dear friends, let us love one another, for love comes from God. Everyone who loves has been born of God and knows God. Whoever does not love does not know God, because God is love.

I John 4:7-8

"You have heard that it was said, 'Love your neighbor and hate your enemy.' But I tell you: Love your enemies and pray for those who persecute you, that you may be sons of your Father in heaven."

Matthew 5:43-45

The Bible tells us to love our neighbors,
and also to love our enemies;
probably because they are generally
the same people.

~ *G. K. Chesterton*

*Dear Father, it makes me feel so sad when I
have broken relationships. Help me, Father,
to love others in the way You love me. Help
me to be kind and considerate instead of
selfish or vindictive. Father, love through me.*

Amen.

Comfort through Love

Knowing you are loved is just about the best thing in the world. A real security comes with love that means you can trust the other person to stick with you, regardless of what happens. Love gives you courage to be yourself, confidence to try new things and energy to involve other people in your life.

Love gives you the strength to face whatever life throws at you. Being loved by others is certainly wonderful.

But the best love of all is God's love. His love is constant and steady. It has no strings attached. It is forgiving. God's love is pure and it makes all other love possible.

Accepting God's love for you and understanding how valuable you are to Him lays a groundwork for accepting love from another person. It also gives you the freedom and ability to love another person. Thank God for His love.

This is how God showed His love among us: He sent His one and only Son into the world that we might live through Him.

I John 4:9

Hope does not disappoint us, because God has poured out His love into our hearts by the Holy Spirit, whom He has given us.

Romans 5:5

How great is the love the Father has lavished on us, that we should be called children of God!

I John 3:1

May the Lord make your love increase and overflow for each other and for everyone else, just as ours does for you.

I Thessalonians 3:12

The LORD is compassionate and gracious, slow to anger, abounding in love.

Psalm 103:8

"By this all men will know that you are My disciples, if you love one another."

John 13:35

"Greater love has no one than this, that he lay down his life for his friends."

John 15:13

No one has ever seen God; but if we love one another, God lives in us and His love is made complete in us.

I John 4:12

God loves us the way we are,
but too much to leave us that way.

~ Leighton Ford

❧

Dear Father, I am constantly amazed by Your love. It is amazing. Your love makes me more loving to those around me. Thank You for Your incredible model of love. Let Your love shine through me to all those in my life.

Amen.

Comfort in Suffering

There are many different kinds of suffering – physical, emotional, even spiritual. One thing they all have in common is that no suffering is pleasant to go through. However, if you know that something good is going to come from suffering – growth, for instance – then it may be easier to endure.

As you're making your way through times of suffering, the need for comfort grows. Comfort will come from those who love you and care about what you're going through.

God places people in your life to surround you with love and care. Did you know that the people around you could be there specifically because God put them in your life to be a comfort and strength for you? Those who know you best and love you most care about what you're going through. Let them minister to you and be a comfort through this time.

Thank God for the comfort He provides.

For Christ's sake, I delight in weaknesses, in insults, in hardships, in persecutions, in difficulties. For when I am weak, then I am strong.

2 Corinthians 12:10

Consider it pure joy, my brothers, whenever you face trials of many kinds, because you know that the testing of your faith develops perseverance.

James 1:2-3

We also rejoice in our sufferings, because we know that suffering produces perseverance; perseverance, character; and character, hope. And hope does not disappoint us, because God has poured out His love into our hearts by the Holy Spirit, whom He has given us.

Romans 5:3-5

Being confident of this, that He who began a good work in you will carry it on to completion until the day of Christ Jesus.

Philippians 1:6

The LORD gives strength to His people; the LORD blesses His people with peace.

Psalm 29:11

"Do not fear, for I am with you; do not be dismayed, for I am your God. I will strengthen you and help you; I will uphold you with My righteous right hand."

Isaiah 41:10

Do not be anxious about anything, but in everything by prayer and petition, with thanksgiving, present your requests to God. And the peace of God, which transcends all understanding, will guard your hearts and your minds in Christ Jesus.

Philippians 4:6-7

Be strong and take heart, all you who hope in the LORD.

Psalm 31:24

*I know God won't give me
anything I can't handle.
I just wish He didn't
trust me so much.*

~ *Mother Teresa*

✦

Dear Father, suffering is so painful because it
is so constant. Help me, Father, to hold on to
You and Your Word to get through this time.
Father, help me to honor You by the way I
deal with this.

Amen.

Comfort in Danger

Aren't our bodies amazing creations? Have you ever experienced the body's warning system of danger? The hairs on the back of your neck tingle, your heart beats faster and your breathing becomes short and hard. Even your skin seems to be on the alert, ready to attack or run. What a system! That's your body's response to danger, but what is your spirit's response? It may vary depending on what the object of fear is.

You may be filled with fear, hopelessness or depression. Of course, your heart's desire is to be rescued, but if that isn't going to happen right away, then you just want to know that you aren't alone. Good news! You're not! God's promise to be with you always holds true even in danger. He's with you. He knows what's going on. Even if you can't feel His presence, you can trust His promise.

You need not fear because nothing will happen to you without His knowledge. He promised to walk beside you – no matter what!

Since we have now been justified by His blood, how much more shall we be saved from God's wrath through Him!

Romans 5:9

"I tell you, do not worry about your life, what you will eat or drink; or about your body, what you will wear. Is not life more important than food, and the body more important than clothes?"

Matthew 6:25

The LORD your God is a merciful God; He will not abandon or destroy you or forget the covenant with your forefathers, which He confirmed to them by oath.

Deuteronomy 4:31

If we are thrown into the blazing furnace, the God we serve is able to save us from it, and He will rescue us from your hand, O king.

Daniel 3:17

I am convinced that neither death nor life, neither angels nor demons, neither the present nor the future, nor any powers, neither height nor depth, nor anything else in all creation, will be able to separate us from the love of God that is in Christ Jesus our Lord.

Romans 8:38-39

I am not ashamed, because I know whom I have believed, and am convinced that He is able to guard what I have entrusted to Him for that day.

2 Timothy 1:12

Vindicate me, O LORD, for I have led a blameless life; I have trusted in the LORD without wavering.

Psalm 26:1

When I am afraid, I will trust in You. In God, whose word I praise, in God I trust; I will not be afraid. What can mortal man do to me?

Psalm 56:3-4

Only he who can say, "The Lord is the strength of my life" can say, "Of whom shall I be afraid?"

~ Alexander MacLaren

❧

Dear Father, sometimes I am afraid ... very afraid. I'm thankful to know that You are with me. I'm glad I'm not alone ... but I'm still afraid. Help me, Father, to trust You with the situation, to depend on You for protection. Comfort me in my fear.

Amen.

Comfort in Discipline

Punishment and discipline are two different things. Discipline is correction. It's a tool to guide you away from disobedience or actions that might hurt you, and point you toward obedience and healthy behavior. God's discipline is not easy to take. In fact, the bottom line is that it hurts – just like most discipline is uncomfortable.

But remember that God disciplines you because He loves you. His desire is for your faith to grow stronger and for your life to be more Christlike.

Yes, discipline is difficult, but try to view it as a learning experience. Ask God to help you learn the lesson He has placed before you. Look for His guidance and trust Him to reveal it. Don't be afraid to ask for prayer support from Christian friends.

Stay in God's Word as you look for guidance and direction. Most of all, thank Him for loving you enough to grow your faith deeper.

Blessed is the man You discipline, O Lord, the man You teach from Your law.

Psalm 94:12

"Those whom I love I rebuke and discipline. So be earnest, and repent. Here I am! I stand at the door and knock. If anyone hears My voice and opens the door, I will come in and eat with him, and he with Me."

Revelation 3:19-20

No discipline seems pleasant at the time, but painful. Later on, however, it produces a harvest of righteousness and peace for those who have been trained by it.

Hebrews 12:11

The fruit of righteousness will be peace; the effect of righteousness will be quietness and confidence forever.

Isaiah 32:17

Endure hardship as discipline; God is treating you as sons. For what son is not disciplined by his father?

Hebrews 12:7

He who spares the rod hates his son, but he who loves him is careful to discipline him.

Proverbs 13:24

All Scripture is God-breathed and is useful for teaching, rebuking, correcting and training in righteousness, so that the man of God may be thoroughly equipped for every good work.

2 Timothy 3:16-17

Teach me to do Your will, for You are my God; may Your good Spirit lead me on level ground.

Psalm 143:10

*Personally I'm always ready to learn,
although I do not always like
being taught.*

~ Winston Churchill

❧

Dear Father, it helps to be reminded that discipline comes because of love. I pray that I won't resent discipline, but will recognize it as Your instruction in my life. Help me, Father, to stay close to You as I learn these lessons and to search Your Word for guidance. Thank You, Father, for loving me enough to discipline me.

Amen.

Passing Comfort On

It's called the domino effect – someone does something kind to you, in gratitude, you turn around and do something kind to someone else; then they pass the kindness on to another, and so on and so on. In this way the love and care of God is passed along to many, many people.

God created us to live in community with one another. Life is not much fun if it is lived in loneliness and isolation. More importantly, we cannot work for God without relating to other people. When you have been given the gift of comfort, love and community, look for ways to pass that along to others. God will give you opportunities to be His hands and His heart to those around you.

There are doubtless many people around you each day who are lonely and hurting and perhaps only need to know that someone cares. Ask God to open your eyes to those to whom you can offer comfort.

A kindhearted woman gains respect, but ruthless men gain only wealth.

Proverbs 11:16

"Your Father in heaven is not willing that any of these little ones should be lost."

Matthew 18:14

Accept one another, then, just as Christ accepted you, in order to bring praise to God.

Romans 15:7

"I was hungry and you gave Me something to eat, I was thirsty and you gave Me something to drink, I was a stranger and you invited Me in, I needed clothes and you clothed Me, I was sick and you looked after Me, I was in prison and you came to visit Me ... The King will reply, 'I tell you the truth, whatever you did for one of the least of these brothers of Mine, you did for Me.'"

Matthew 25:35-36, 40

Do not forget to entertain strangers, for by so doing some people have entertained angels without
knowing it.

Hebrews 13:2

Dear friends, let us love one another, for love comes
from God. Everyone who loves has been born of God
and knows God.

1 John 4:7

Dear friends, since God so loved us, we also ought
to love one another. No one has ever seen God;
but if we love one another, God lives in us and His
love is made complete in us.

1 John 4:11-12

This is my prayer: that your love may abound more
and more in knowledge and depth of insight, so
that you may be able to discern what is best and
may be pure and blameless until the day of Christ,
filled with the fruit of righteousness that comes
through Jesus Christ – to the glory and praise of
God.

Philippians 1:9-11

Kind words can be short and easy to speak, but their echoes are truly endless.
~ *Mother Teresa*

Dear Father, I so appreciate every word of comfort and every act of kindness that comes my way. Let me never forget to pass those acts of kindness on. Father, open my eyes to those around me who need comfort and kindness, and help me to be the one who offers it in Your name.

Amen.

Comfort as Christ Did

The greatest example of comfort-giving is Christ Himself. Read through the Gospels and observe how He related to people. Pay attention to those whom He spent time with. It was often the hurting, ill or grief-stricken. Jesus reached out to those who needed comfort.

Sometimes life gets so busy that we only have time for those in our "inner circle". Those family members or friends to whom we are closest are the ones we offer our care to. Meanwhile, co-workers or neighbors who need the comfort of our time – a cup of coffee, a walk in the park, playtime with children while we chat – are overlooked.

Jesus was so often pressed on all sides by crowds of people who wanted something from Him; yet, He kept working, teaching and healing until all their needs were met. He didn't just reach out to the important or to the people He knew, He went to those who needed Him.

"Blessed are the merciful, for they will be shown mercy."

Matthew 5:7

"Let your light shine before men, that they may see your good deeds and praise your Father in heaven."

Matthew 5:16

This is my prayer: that your love may abound more and more in knowledge and depth of insight, so that you may be able to discern what is best and may be pure and blameless until the day of Christ, filled with the fruit of righteousness that comes through Jesus Christ – to the glory and praise of God.

Philippians 1:9-11

"Give to the one who asks you, and do not turn away from the one who wants to borrow from you."

Matthew 5:42

"In everything, do to others what you would have them do to you, for this sums up the Law and the Prophets."

Matthew 7:12

"I am the vine; you are the branches. If a man remains in Me and I in him, he will bear much fruit; apart from Me you can do nothing."

John 15:5

"Love the Lord your God with all your heart and with all your soul and with all your mind. This is the first and greatest commandment. And the second is like it: 'Love your neighbor as yourself.'"

Matthew 22:37-39

"Do not seek revenge or bear a grudge against one of your people, but love your neighbor as yourself. I am the LORD."

Leviticus 19:18

If a man does not make new acquaintance as he advances through life, he will soon find himself left alone.

~ Samuel Johnson

Dear Father, I desire more than anything to live my life in a way that reflects Jesus to others. Help me, Father, to notice those around me who need comfort and then help me to do what I can to help them.

Amen.